A Walk with Jesus

(A True Story)

By

Lorenzo Smith

Contents

Dedication

Dedicated to my mother Geraldine Banfield! Thank you mom for always keeping me spiritually conscious, and grounded! Always teaching me about God and Christ! I love you and hope to see you again in the after life!

Acknowledgments

I would like to acknowledge my Lord and savior Jesus Christ! I've always believed in the Lord, but now I can say I know him! He really heard my cry in a time in my life when I was very much lost and confused! I prayed in tears for the Lord to reveal himself to me and he did! I'm forever grateful, thankful, and joyful for Jesus Christ love! Thank you very much Father God in heaven for blessing me with your precious presence, and for sending your only begotten son that whosoever believeth shall not perish, but have everlasting life Amen!

About the Author

Grew up with four brothers being raised by a single mom in Compton California and Las Angeles California! The fourth of five boys! Mom was married a few times and she always took care of her son's Donald, Travis, Jeffrey, Marquette, and myself Lorenzo! I was a professional boxer, but due to getting in trouble with the law my pro career was cut short! Had a daughter at 19 years of age, then a son at 22 I was a single father for a while, kids are grown and now I have 3 grandkids! Now living in Vegas and I'm a member of True Love Missionary Baptist Church!

Introduction

Encountering Jesus Christ is a profound and life-altering experience that has the potential to transform one's perspective on faith, spirituality, and the world at large. As I reflect upon my personal encounter with Jesus, I am compelled to share this extraordinary event through the written word in this book. I will explore the reasons why I want to write about meeting Jesus Christ and the impact it has had on my life.

The Significance of The Encounter

Meeting Jesus Christ is a deeply personal and spiritual experience that transcends the boundaries of ordinary human existence. It was a moment of divine connection, where one feels the presence of a higher power and experiences a profound sense of love, peace, and purpose. By writing about this encounter, I hope to convey the magnitude of this experience and its transformative effect on my life.

Sharing the message of Hope and Redemption

Jesus Christ is often regarded as a symbol of hope, love, and redemption. Through his teachings and actions, he exemplified compassion, forgiveness, and selflessness. By writing about my encounter with Jesus, I aim to share this message of hope and redemption with others. In a world filled with turmoil, despair, and uncertainty, reminding people of the power of faith and the possibility of spiritual renewal is crucial.

Inspiring Others on Their Spiritual Journey

Each person's spiritual journey is unique, and encountering Jesus Christ can be a catalyst for profound personal growth and transformation. By sharing my own experience, I hope to inspire others on their own spiritual journeys. Writing about meeting Jesus allows me to offer guidance, support, and encouragement to those who may be seeking a deeper connection with their faith or searching for answers to life's existential questions.

Preserving the Memory for Future Generations

The memory of meeting Jesus Christ is a precious and sacred one that deserves to be preserved for future generations. By writing about this encounter, I can ensure that the details and significance of this experience are not lost over time. It becomes a testament to the enduring power of faith and serves as a source of inspiration for future generations.

The Power of Testimony

Sharing personal testimonies has long been a powerful tool for spreading the message of faith and spirituality. By writing about my encounter with Jesus, I can contribute to this tradition of testimony, offering a firsthand account of the impact of encountering the divine. Testimonies can touch hearts, challenge beliefs, and ignite a spark of curiosity and exploration in others.

Chapter 1

Proverbs 22:6 Train up a Child

Thanks to my mom, I've always been spiritually inclined! She always quoted the bible, so I knew a lot about Jesus at an early age! I always believed in the stories of the bible, but never would I have ever believed that I would meet him! I've heard many people say he's coming back, but I'm here to tell you he's already here. At a time in my life when I was very depressed and going through what seemed like a midlife crisis, I called out to God and asked Jesus if he could please come see me so I could truly know him! At this time, to be honest, I was contemplating suicide! I believe in my heart that Jesus heard my prayer because I prostrated myself before him, and he felt my pain! After my fervent prayer that night, I felt a great sense of relief. I think after all the trials, tribulations, and turmoil I had been going through, I needed to cry! Months later, I would have an encounter with someone I perceived to be the creator of all things. It wasn't just Jesus that I met that night. I also met Peter and John! I know this Testimony may be hard to believe, so I plan to take a lie-detector test to prove that it's true. Anyone who has encountered Jesus' weather in person as I did, in a vision, or in a dream would probably say the most extraordinary thing about him is his beautiful eyes! I live in Las Vegas, but I'm from Los Angeles, California. My upbringing was rough, but my mom always made sure I and my brothers knew about God and Jesus Christ. Church did not stop me and my siblings from getting involved with gangs and drugs because it was always around us. I have always felt a strong spiritual connection with God since a young age, but the world has a way of making one lose faith in a higher power. God also has a way of getting us to listen. Sometimes, we think things are going so badly, but if we trust in God and Jesus, things will really work out! It's about having pure faith in his ability to pull us through. He is the author and finisher of our faith. Sometimes, when my mom would miss church, she would give me the tides to take to church! I would sit and listen to the preacher! I got baptized at about 12, but by the age of sixteen, I was going to juvenile corrections for grand theft auto. I understand now that God's presence doesn't stop the devil from trying to throw one of the paths that God has ordained for you. Life has taken me on so many journeys, some good and some bad, but it has always ultimately led me back to repentance. My pastor preached a sermon on Matthew 25 about the master who went on a journey, and before leaving, he entrusted his three servants with talents! The Bible says he gave them each according to their ability, however the one with the least did the least with it. We all have God-given talents, which we all will have to account for on the day of judgement! Meeting Jesus and his two disciples has opened a whole new spiritual world to me, and I now understand it is not about the talents God has given me but what I do with them. If I seek to honor God and to be a beacon to others, God will increase my talents just as he did the servant in Matthew 25v20.

Jesus said his sheep will know him and follow him! This is also true for his disciples. On the night of my divine encounter, I first recognized Peter, and I knew exactly who he was. It was only days after I lay on my bed with a gun in my hand, praying to God to please show me that he really exists! Jesus really heard my prayers. When I first glanced at Saint Peter, somehow, I knew he was from heaven! I kept repeating is this real? Is this real? Peter looked to his left at another gentleman, shaking his head yes, and when I looked at the other person, I immediately knew it was Saint John. I can't tell you how I knew exactly who these two men were, but I did! In tears, I tried to hug Saint John! He gently deflected me and pointed me to a third man who beckoned me towards him. His eyes seemed to hold the weight of the world in them! I felt my sin leave me and rest on him! My first words to him were am I forgiven? He replied yes, and I asked what I had to do to get to heaven. He said nothing, just do what you're doing! As we walked, the air seemed charged with an otherworldly energy! In recent years, I learned that Jesus' Hebrew name is Yahshua or Yahoshua, and even though I knew I was walking with the divine charismatic teacher and had just had a profound encounter with two of his devoted followers, I was compelled to ask, what is your name? He said I am Jesus Christ. I did not know when I woke up that morning that my path was about to intersect with the divine. Since then, my life has truly changed! I realize now that this life is just a blow in the wind. My experience was divine; however, I still struggle with my sinful nature! The difference is that I now know that God and Jesus are real, and they love me with a love that could not be fathomed in the world we live in. At this time in my life, I don't have much, but I wouldn't trade places with anyone in the world, no matter how rich, because I understand now that every house has a builder, but the one who builds everything is God, and unless the Lord builds the house, its builder's labor in vain.

Chapter 2

Proverbs 9:10 Fear of the Lord is the beginning of wisdom.

My purpose in writing about this encounter is to share the message. I now have a newfound sense of purpose that emerged from this divine encounter. The encounter with Peter and John, followed by the presence of Jesus himself, represents a profound spiritual connection. I felt an overwhelming sense of peace, love, and divine guidance that enveloped me! The spiritual aura that surrounded Peter, John, and Jesus was filled with transformative power. I think it would be impossible for me to convey the spiritual connection I experienced with them. It was a life-altering experience that defies conventional explanation. The urge to indulge in sinful behavior does not dissipate. However, now I'm aware! Jesus said forgive them, Father, for they know not what they do! I could see everything in his eyes: love, concern, and empathy. His eyes are the most beautiful eyes I have ever seen! They pierced the innermost parts of my soul, and I knew that he knew everything about me and that he really loved me! It was also a great fear that came over me when I first met him. Somehow, I understood this man had the power to send me to hell or save me. Maybe that's why my first words to him were, am I forgiven?" Proverbs

9:10 says fear of the Lord is the beginning of wisdom, and knowledge of the Holy One is understanding! This is now one of my favorite verses in the bible. I felt that fear, and I spiritually discerned he was the Holy one it was referring to.

After that night, I went home still in disbelief at what I had just experienced! I only told people who are very close to me, and I thank God that I was able to tell my mother, who just recently passed away because she is responsible for the little faith I had! Her response was, "Baby, you don't know that you were supposed to be a preacher?" I always knew that my mother was spiritually gifted. She raised five boys on her own, and I can't remember ever being hungry or without life's necessities. She would say things like be that as it may, and God made you the head and not the tail! I'm really going to miss her guidance, but I know for sure she is with the Almighty Father in heaven. Love is the foundation of life itself! God so loved the world that he gave his only begotten son that whosoever believes in him should not perish but have everlasting life! The devil works through fear, but if God be with me, whom or what shall I fear? The second question I asked Jesus was what do I have to do to get to heaven? He replied nothing, just do what you're doing! I realize today that God's grace and forgiveness are a gift, and the only thing that is required is faith!

Chapter 3

Psalms 143:6 I stretch forth my hands.

There I am, in the neon-lit heart of Las Vegas, where fortunes are made and lost on the roll of dice! I did not just stumble upon an encounter that would render the shimmering lights trivial. It was meant to happen! The thought of meeting someone who lived over two millennia ago is statistically impossible, yet there I stood, face to face with Saint Peter, the beloved disciple of Jesus Christ himself! What does it mean when the impossible shatters the foundation of what we believe to be true? After my repeating, is this real? He gestured toward another figure. My heart understood before my mind could catch up that this was Saint John, another beloved disciple of Jesus Christ! Peter looked to be in his late twenties or early thirties; he had a full beard and short curly hair, and they were jet black! I could tell he was Jewish, but he could have passed for Spanish with his olive skin tone! John, to my surprise, was a black man about five nine, thine stature, and I could feel he was a serious nonsense type of person. The tears that followed were not of sorrow but of joy, an awakening. I understand why John did not allow me to hug him. He understood I was not there to see them, but the messiah himself! John pointed. I turned then and saw him, a man whose presence seemed to hush the roar of Vegas into a distant echo, just as he had rebuked the winds and the waves in Matthew 8. It was completely calm! I was like one of those disciples who went and woke him, saying save me! I was losing faith! When he stretched forth his hand and beckoned me to come, just as the wind and waves of Matthew 8:26, I became completely calm.

In every life, there are moments when the veil of ordinary existence is peeled back to reveal a glimpse of the extraordinary. This is the account of such a moment in my life! An experience so profound and surreal that to speak of it invites disbelief, yet to remain silent is to deny the very essence of my being. What is our purpose if we do not seek and embrace the truth, no matter how implausible it may appear? Why should this matter to you, the reader? Because in an age where digital screens dictate reality and cynicism often clouds our vision, we are all searching for something authentic, something transcendent that reconnects us with the essence of what it means to be truly alive. This is not merely a recounting of an otherworldly encounter; it is an invitation to open your mind to the possibility that there is more to this world than meets the eye. A chance to delve into the depths of faith, scepticism, and wonder. I am inviting you to explore the significance of an encounter with the divine in the most unexpected of places.

Chapter 4

1 John 4:13-15 Hereby know we that we dwell in him!

Fremont Street was a symphony of neon lights that cascaded from the vaulted canopy above. A technological marvel that bathed the bustling crowd below on an artificial day. The air was charged with the sounds of laughter, the clinking of glasses, and the siren call of slot machines. The street stretched before me like a river of lights, its banks lined with towering casinos and shops, each vying for attention with their signs and promises of fortune. While walking with my Lord, I did not notice anything going on around us! My soul felt the warmth of spiritual nourishment! The question lingered, suspended in my mind: how does one find the divine in a land dedicated to the fleeting and the superficial? I did not find him. He found me, for I was the one who was missing. Everything seemed to have stood still, allowing the wave of humanity to flow around me. Each person was like a story unto themselves. In the heart of this sensory onslaught, I felt an unexpected peace, a tranquility that seemed out of place amid the chaos. It emanated from the figure beside me. I felt like I was walking with my best friend, whose eyes held the depth of the ages, a testament to the trials and triumphs of faith. His visage was illuminated not by the flashing lights but by a soft, ethereal glow that seemed to come from within, a divine radiance that outshone the artificial brilliance of the boulevard.

I turned to face him, and in his gaze, I found an invitation to see beyond the surface, to perceive the world with a clarity that transcends the ordinary. "What is your name?" I asked, his voice like a gentle nudge against the tide of my thoughts, and he replied I am Jesus Christ. I pondered the question, realizing I already knew the answer. I just needed him to say it! My journey was not just a physical walk down a neon-lit street but a pilgrimage through the landscapes of my own soul.

Now that I have read the Bible more and returned to the church, I realize Peter and John were together in many of the Bible stories! Each one of them carries within them the spark of divine grace. Many are unaware because we are blinded by the pursuit of things that glitter but do not enlighten. The contrast between the two worlds, the material and the spiritual, was never clearer to me than at that moment. I felt like the glittering Boulevard, with all its splendor, was a mirage, a beautiful illusion that promised much but satisfied little. And there I was, walking amid the illusion with the embodiment of truth, a beacon of a different kind! There is more to our existence than what can be seen, touched, or purchased. There is a realm where the soul is nourished, where the transient gives way to the eternal, and where the truest riches are found not in the clatter of coins but in the quiet spaces of the spirit.

Chapter 5

Matthew 13: The Parable of the Sower

With each step I took alongside this modern manifestation of Jesus, I was reminded that the core message was that of love, compassion, and redemption that transcends time. The human heart is the canvas upon which the sacred paints its masterpiece. Jesus spoke in parables that mirror the timeless yet resonate with the pulse of today. His very presence tells of a network, not of wires and waves, but of shared humanity and the connections that bind us beyond the superficial ties of social media. His words are simple and profound, cutting through the complexities of life and reminding me that amidst our endless striving and accumulation, there is beauty in simplicity, a truth that requires no embellishment, only faith. After meeting Jesus, I experienced a profound awakening of my spirit. I no longer see things as they are supposed to be but as they are! My perception of the world, myself, and my purpose has shifted. When I asked Jesus what I had to do to get to heaven, he replied, nothing, just do what you're doing! I didn't understand what that meant because I hadn't been doing anything. John 13:14 says if then, your Lord and master, have washed your feet; ye also ought to wash one another's feet. He washed not only my feet but my whole body! He cleansed me of sin. Therefore, I should love others as he loves me and forgive as I have been forgiven! It is a newfound understanding of God's love and grace, and it has completely transformed my perspective on life. Walking in faith is not without its challenges. I still have doubts, struggles, and questions, but Jesus has granted me the faith it takes to seek answers, and I find solace in the teachings of Jesus and the wisdom of scripture.

Meeting Jesus face to face has ignited a process of transformation within me and has changed my character, values, and priorities because of my evolved faith. I now seek growth through forgiveness and the pursuit of righteousness. My hope is to deepen my relationship with Jesus as my walk of faith progresses. I found a great church here in Las Vegas called true love missionary Baptist church! I attend almost every Sunday, and I now pray every day as soon as I open my eyes! Through prayer, meditation, scripture study and other transformative practices, I hope to cultivate a more intimate connection with my Lord and Savior. As followers of Jesus, we are called to share the good news of his love and salvation! Through evangelism and other various ways, we can effectively share our faith with others and provide practical guidance and insights on how we all can grow closer to our higher power.

Chapter 6

Psalm :119 Blessed are they whose ways are blameless.

In a world filled with chaos and uncertainty, many of us find ourselves yearning for something more profound and meaningful. We seek answers to questions that seem to elude us, searching for a purpose that transcends the mundane. In life inevitable challenges will arise on our spiritual journey! We achieve spiritual growth through adversity and learn the importance of resilience, continually learning lessons from facing our fears. There will always be obstacles to overcome, but understanding the significance of surrendering to the divine and trusting the process is the most important part of the journey. In Mark 9:23, Jesus says all things are possible for one who believes. His disciples could not cast out an evil spirit from a little boy, not because of lack of faith, but because some can only come out through prayer and fasting! There are various ways in which we can connect with the divine! Faith is significant, and exploring our different religious and spiritual traditions helps us to cultivate a personal relationship with the divine. Prayer and fasting are very important to this process of finding our own unique path to God. Embark with me on a remarkable journey that takes us beyond the physical realm and into the depths of our souls. This path is about embracing life as a spiritual journey, and hopefully, this book can serve as a guide to help navigate the intricacies of this profound expedition.

Awakening to the call is a process in which I explore the catalysts that have awakened my spiritual yearnings. The moment of epiphany, the encounter that shook me to the core, and the realization that there is more to life than meets the eye. I've always felt the presence of Jesus but didn't really know what I was feeling. Through meditation, mindfulness, Prayer, and other practices, we can connect with our inner selves and the divine.

Thanks to Jesus restoring my faith, I am now in the process of exploring the depths of my inner self. The importance of self-awareness, emotional healing, and the process of letting go of past traumas. I think about the power of forgiveness, gratitude, and cultivating a positive mindset as I navigate the complexities of my inner landscape. Mark 11:22-23 says to have faith in God. Truly I tell you if anyone says to this mountain, go, be cast into the sea, and does not doubt in their heart but believes that what they say will happen, it will be done for them. In the next chapter I will tell you about the inevitable challenges that I have faced on what I now know to be my spiritual journey.

Chapter 7

Proverbs 13:20 He that walketh with wise men shall be wise

After meeting Jesus Christ face to face, one's life is forever changed. The experience of being in the presence of the Son of God is indescribable and overwhelming. One is filled with a deep sense of love, joy, and peace that surpasses all understanding. This encounter with Jesus brings about a transformation in one's heart and mind. It ignites a newfound passion for living a life of purpose and dedicating oneself to following Jesus's teachings. There is a renewed sense of hope and faith, knowing that Jesus is always with us, guiding and protecting us. However, to be honest, it did not take away my sinful nature, yet now I'm always aware of my sin! Jesus restored my faith when I needed him most. This encounter brings about a sense of humility and gratitude as one realizes the magnitude of Jesus' sacrifice for our sins. Life after meeting Jesus face to face becomes a journey of continuously growing in faith and deepening one's relationship with him. It brings about a desire to share this life-changing experience with others, spreading the message of God's love and salvation. Ultimately, meeting Jesus fills one's life with unexplainable joy and fulfillment that can only come from experiencing the presence of the Son of God.

After meeting Jesus Christ, my life was completely transformed. The encounter filled me with a sense of awe and wonder as I gazed upon the loving and compassionate eyes of my savior. I felt a deep sense of peace and joy that I had never experienced before. My heart was filled with love and forgiveness, and all my worries and fears seemed to vanish in His presence. I was overwhelmed with the realization that He died for my sins. And was with me always, guiding me on my journey. From that moment on, I felt a strong desire to follow His teachings and live my life in accordance with His will. I'm still fighting temptations because that devil will not stop trying to lead us astray. However, my faith is restored, and I know that if I have Jesus, no weapon formed against me shall prosper. The encounter with Jesus changed my perspective on life, and I found a new purpose and meaning in serving others and spreading His message of love and salvation. I no longer felt lost, but I was still alone. I tried to find a companion, but the one I found was full of worldliness, and she would never go to church with me! Now I realize I have a constant companion in Jesus, who gave me strength and courage to face any challenges that came my way. Meeting Jesus face to face truly transformed my life, and I am forever grateful for the profound impact it had on my heart and soul.

In a world filled with allure and distraction, the path of faith often seems narrow and treacherous, yet for those who dare to embark on this spiritual journey, the rewards are boundless. I am struggling to navigate the complexities of life while staying true to my faith. As I set out on my quest, I encounter temptations and sins that threaten to derail me from the righteous path. I find myself at a crossroads, faced with a choice that could alter the course of my life. Temptation whispers sweet promises in my ear, urging me to abandon my beliefs in favor of temporary gratification. As I grapple with this internal struggle, I must find the strength within myself to resist the siren call of sin. I met someone after being single for three years, and after she moved in, she told me she was married but separated! In the depths of my soul, a fierce battle was raging between light and darkness. I was torn between the familiar comfort of sin, lust, and adultery and the unfamiliar terrain of faith. As I wrestle with my inner demons, I learn that true strength comes from surrendering to a higher power and trusting in divine guidance. After six months, she proved to be disloyal. Let's just say God opened my eyes and put me back on the path of righteousness.

With each step forward, I grow stronger in my faith, learning to lean on my church family and draw inspiration from the stories of those who have walked this path before me. Through prayer, reflection, and unwavering determination, I will find the courage to face my temptations head-on. As I push toward the end of my journey, I will emerge transformed and renewed. Jesus has helped me discover the power of faith to overcome even the darkest of temptations. With a heart full of gratitude and a spirit fortified by Jesus himself, I will practice resilience as I set out to share my story with others who may be struggling on their own paths.

Chapter 8

James 4:6. God Opposes the proud but gives grace unto the humble

Living a Godly life and striving to stay away from sin is now my goal. I must cultivate my virtues, such as love, compassion, honesty, humility, and self-control, while actively working to avoid actions that are considered by God to be sinful, especially sexual immorality. Here are some key principles that we can use to live a Godly life and stay away from sin! Develop a relationship with Jesus. If you believe in God as your higher power, nurturing a connection with Jesus will provide guidance, strength, and motivation to live a virtuous life. Regularly reflect on your thoughts, words, and actions to identify areas where you may be falling short. Acknowledge your mistakes, and transgressions in prayer, repent, and God will forgive you! The Bible offers guidance on living a righteous life. Engage with it regularly to strengthen your understanding of God's word, ethical principles, and moral values. Engage in prayer daily to cultivate inner peace, spiritual clarity, and strength. This will also provide you with an opportunity to seek guidance, express gratitude, and repent. Surround yourself with individuals who share the same spiritual values and can offer support and encouragement on your spiritual journey.

Practice forgiveness, both towards others and yourself. I've decided that holding on to grudges and resentment can only hinder my spiritual growth. By practicing forgiveness, I can cultivate compassion and peace in my heart as I strive to embody virtues such as love, kindness, honesty, and all the other fruits of the spirit mentioned in Galatians 5:22-23. I believe that Jesus gave me the gift of discernment to identify situations, habits, and influences that may lead me toward sinful behavior, but I must take the necessary steps to avoid or overcome them. I have a mindset of gratitude for the blessings in my life, both big and small. My kids, my grandchildren, and my truck. Gratitude can shift our focus away from negative emotions and temptations, helping us stay grounded in our spiritual values. Remember that living a Godly life is a journey that requires continuous effort, self-awareness, spiritual awareness, and commitment. Nobody is perfect, and everyone makes mistakes, the key is to learn from them, seek forgiveness, and strive to align your thoughts and actions with Jesus Christ. Cultivate a mindset of love, compassion, and integrity, and together, we can walk the path of righteousness and experience the deepest sense of fulfillment and peace in this life and the life to come.

Chapter 9

Mark 14:27 You Will All Fall Away

Today in church, I found myself fighting back tears as my pastor preached a sermon he called correction in the courtyard. It was about the disciple Simon Peter. In Mark 14:29, he told Jesus that even if everyone else fell away, he would not! In the next verse, Jesus told Peter today, you will deny me three times before the cock crows twice. I reflected on the day I met Jesus and remembered Peter was the first person I saw that day, and somehow, I knew exactly who he was. My pastor talked about how, in the courtyard, while Jesus was being sacrificed, people confronted Peter about being with Jesus, and just as the Messiah had said, peter denied him three times. Jesus did not love Peter any less because he knew his intentions when he said he would die if he had to. God created the heavens and the earth, and with great love, He formed humanity in his own image. From that moment on, a bond of love was established that would transcend time and space. As history unfolded, man strayed away from God's perfect love, but his love remained constant and unwavering. Through times of joy and times of sorrow, God's love will shine brightly, offering hope and redemption to all who seek him. In the ultimate display of love, God sent his only son, Jesus Christ, who still walks among humanity, to show the depths of his love. Now I understand Hebrews 13:1-3 Remember to entertain strangers, for some have entertained angels unawares. Through his life, teachings, and sacrifice on the cross, Jesus demonstrates the lengths to which God would go to express his love for humanity. Through Jesus Christ, humanity was offered redemption and a path back to God's loving embrace. No matter how far we may stray, God's love is always there, ready to welcome us home with open arms.

As we embrace God's love for us, we are called to love one another in return. Through acts of kindness, compassion, and forgiveness, we can reflect God's love for the world around us and make a positive impact on those we encounter. God's love knows no bounds and extends into eternity. As we journey through this life, we can take comfort in the knowledge that God's love will never fail us and that we are destined for an eternity in His presence. As we close this book, I pray we always remember that God's love for humanity is a love that endures forever. Through every trial and triumph, God's love remains constant and unwavering, guiding us on our journey through life and into eternity. Walking with Jesus through Sin City is a testament to the boundless love God has for humanity. A love that transcends all understanding and offers hope, redemption, and eternal life to all who seek it. May this book serve as a reminder of God's love for each one of us to live in love and walk in the light of His grace. Amen.

Chapter 10

Psalms 19:13 keep back also thy servant from presumptuous sins

This story is still playing out as I navigate through the intricacies of life. Lessons get deeper, and my faith grows stronger. We are all human, with carnal thoughts and actions! To flee fornication, I set out to find a wife because God's word says in 1 Corinthians 7v1 that it is good for a man not to touch a woman, but to avoid fornication, let every man have his wife, and every woman her husband. In this chapter, I would like to talk about Idolatry. In the journey of faith, one of the most profound challenges humanity faces is the temptation of idolatry. Idolatry, at its core, is the act of giving worship or undue reverence to something or someone other than God. Throughout history, civilizations and individuals have wrestled with this concept, often blurring the lines between true devotion to the Creator and the allure of created things. Idolatry manifests in various forms, both overt and subtle. In ancient times, people fashioned physical idols from wood, stone, or precious metals, believing these objects held divine power or represented gods. However, idolatry extends far beyond mere statues. Today, it encompasses anything that consumes our hearts and minds more than God Himself: wealth, success, relationships, ideologies, and even one's own desires and ambitions.

The essence of idolatry lies not only in what we worship but in where we place our trust and ultimate loyalty. When anything besides God takes center stage in our lives, whether consciously or unconsciously, it becomes an idol, this can lead to spiritual disconnection, distortion of priorities, and a gradual erosion of our relationship with the true source of life and meaning.

Effects on Our Walk with God

1. Spiritual Distraction and Division

Idolatry divides our allegiance. Instead of wholeheartedly seeking God, we become divided between Him and worldly pursuits. Jesus warned, "No one can serve two masters. Either you will hate the one and love the other, or you will be devoted to the one and despise the other" (Matthew 6:24, NIV). Idolatry dilutes our spiritual focus, leaving us spiritually adrift and less sensitive to the leading of the Holy Spirit.

1. **Erosion of True Worship**

True worship springs from a heart surrendered to God in spirit and truth (John 4:24). Idolatry substitutes this authentic worship with rituals, traditions, or even self-serving acts aimed at appeasing false gods or ideologies. As idols replace God in our affections, genuine communion with Him diminishes, leaving us spiritually malnourished and disconnected.

1. **Distortion of Identity and Purpose**

Idolatry distorts our understanding of who we are in relation to God. It defines us by what we possess or achieve rather than by our identity as children of God. This distortion leads to a relentless pursuit of worldly success, recognition, or material gain, often at the expense of our spiritual health and well-being. Our purpose becomes skewed, centered on fulfilling selfish desires rather than aligning with God's will and kingdom purposes.

1. **Hindrance to Transformation**

The process of sanctification, becoming more like Christ, is hindered by idolatry. Instead of allowing God to shape and mold us, idols imprison us in cycles of pride, greed, fear, and self-sufficiency. The apostle Paul cautioned, "Put to death, therefore, whatever belongs to your earthly nature: sexual immorality, impurity, lust, evil desires and greed, which is idolatry" (Colossians 3:5, NIV). Idolatry prevents the transformative work of the Holy Spirit from fully renewing our minds and hearts.

Overcoming Idolatry

Overcoming idolatry begins with recognizing its presence in our lives and repenting before God. It requires a deliberate shift in focus—placing God at the center of our affections, pursuits, and decisions. This involves:

- **Cultivating a Heart of Worship:** Devoting ourselves to genuine worship and intimacy with God through prayer, study of His Word, and fellowship with other believers.

- **Renewing Our Minds:** Allowing the truth of God's Word to reshape our perspectives, priorities, and desires.

- **Surrendering Control:** Yielding our ambitions, fears, and possessions to God's sovereignty and guidance.

- **Accountability and Community:** Surrounding ourselves with fellow believers who encourage and challenge us in our walk with God.

Conclusion

Idolatry is not merely a historical artifact but a pervasive challenge in the contemporary spiritual landscape. Its insidious influence can subtly infiltrate even the most devout hearts. Yet, through awareness, prayer, and intentional pursuit of God, we can guard against its allure and experience the freedom and fulfillment found only in wholehearted devotion to Him. As we journey deeper into our relationship with God, may we continually examine our hearts, casting aside every idol and surrendering ourselves fully to the One who alone is worthy of our worship and adoration.

Chapter 11

James 1:6 But let him ask in Faith nothing wavering

In the journey of following Jesus Christ, faith stands as the foundational cornerstone upon which everything else rests. It is through faith that we embark on a transformative relationship with Him, one that transcends mere belief into a dynamic, life-altering commitment.

Understanding Faith

Hebrews 11:1 beautifully defines faith as "the assurance of things hoped for, the conviction of things not seen." It is this deep conviction, this unwavering trust in the promises of God, that propels us forward in our walk with Jesus. Faith is not passive; rather, it is active and resolute, shaping our thoughts, actions, and perspectives.

Trusting in God's Promises

When we choose to follow Jesus Christ, we are called to surrender ourselves completely to His will and purpose. This surrender is not blind but informed by the promises laid out in His Word. **Jeremiah 29:11** assures us of God's plans for our welfare and not for harm, to give us a future with hope.

Such promises require faith to embrace fully, especially in times of uncertainty and challenge.

Walking in Obedience

Faith in Jesus Christ manifests itself in obedience to His teachings and commandments. **John 14:15** declares, "If you love me, you will keep my commandments." This obedience stems from a deep-rooted trust that God's ways are perfect and His guidance leads to abundant life. It requires us to surrender our own desires and submit to His will, believing that His wisdom far surpasses our own.

Overcoming Doubt and Adversity

Throughout our journey, doubts and adversities may arise, challenging the steadfastness of our faith. Yet, **James 1:6** encourages us to ask in faith, without doubting, for the one who doubts is like a wave of the sea that is driven and tossed by the wind. Faith allows us to withstand these storms, knowing that God is faithful to His promises and His strength is made perfect in our weakness (**2 Corinthians 12:9**).

The Power of Faith in Transformation

Above all, faith in Jesus Christ brings about transformation. **2 Corinthians 5:17 tells** us that if anyone is in Christ, they are a new creation. This transformation is not superficial but a profound change of heart and mind, shaping our character to reflect the love, grace, and truth of Christ to the world around us.

Living by Faith

Living by faith means actively trusting in God's provision, guidance, and promises each day. It means seeking His kingdom first (**Matthew 6:33**) acknowledging our dependence on Him for every aspect of our lives. As we walk this journey of faith, we are reminded that it is not by our own strength but by His Spirit that we are able to follow Jesus Christ faithfully.

In conclusion, faith is not an optional accessory but an essential element in the life of every believer. It is the catalyst that ignites our relationship with Jesus Christ, sustains us through trials, and empowers us to live according to His will. May we continually grow in faith, trusting in the One who called us out of darkness into His marvelous light (**1 Peter 2:9**), and may our lives be a testimony to His faithfulness and grace. Amen!

Chapter 12

Genesis 18:14 Is there anything too hard for the Lord?

In the teachings of Christianity, adultery is addressed with profound seriousness, rooted in the sacredness of marriage and the ethical framework of God's commandments. This chapter delves into the Christian perspective on adultery, highlighting its spiritual, moral, and relational implications.

Understanding Adultery in Biblical Context

The Bible, particularly in the Old and New Testaments, provides clear guidance on the sanctity of marriage and the consequences of adultery. In the Ten Commandments, God commands, "You shall not commit adultery" (Exodus 20:14), emphasizing fidelity within the covenant of marriage as integral to honoring God's design for human relationships.

1. Betrayal of Covenant: Adultery is viewed as a betrayal of the covenant established between spouses and God Himself. Marriage, according to Christian teaching, is a sacred union intended to reflect the faithful, unconditional love of Christ for His Church (Ephesians 5:22-33). Adultery disrupts this divine purpose, severing the trust and unity intended within marriage.

2. Spiritual Consequences: Beyond its relational and emotional impact, adultery is considered a sin against God. Jesus reaffirmed the seriousness of adultery, teaching that even looking at another person with lustful intent constitutes adultery in the heart (Matthew 5:27-28). This underscores the importance of purity not only in actions but also in thoughts and intentions.

3. Restoration and Forgiveness: While adultery is condemned, Christian teaching also emphasizes the possibility of forgiveness and restoration through genuine repentance and reconciliation (1 John 1:9). This process involves sincere remorse, accountability, and a commitment to amend behavior, seeking forgiveness from God and the injured spouse.

The Importance of Fidelity in Christian Marriage

Christianity places a high value on fidelity within marriage, viewing it as a reflection of God's faithfulness and love. Fidelity promotes unity, trust, and mutual support, allowing couples to experience the blessings of a harmonious relationship grounded in Christ's teachings.

1. Covenantal Commitment: Marriage is viewed as a covenantal commitment before God, where spouses pledge to love, honor, and cherish each other until death parts them (Mark 10:6-9). Fidelity within this covenant serves as a

testimony to God's enduring faithfulness and strengthens the marital bond.

2. Honoring God's Design: By honoring fidelity, couples uphold God's design for marriage—a union that reflects His unchanging love and commitment. This commitment extends beyond mere emotional satisfaction to encompass spiritual growth, sacrificial love, and mutual respect.

3. Seeking Guidance and Support: Christian couples are encouraged to seek guidance from Scripture, prayer, and wise counsel within their faith community to navigate challenges and temptations that may threaten fidelity. Accountability and fellowship provide strength and encouragement in upholding marital vows.

Facing Temptations with Faith

In a world marked by temptations and cultural shifts, Christians are called to uphold biblical values and resist the allure of adultery through faith and reliance on God's grace.

1. Renewing the Mind: Christians are urged to renew their minds through Scripture and prayer, guarding against the influences of a secular culture that may trivialize or condone infidelity (Romans 12:2).

2. Strengthening Marital Unity: Couples can strengthen their marital unity by prioritizing communication, intimacy,

and mutual respect. Building a Christ-centered relationship fosters resilience against external pressures that threaten fidelity.

3. Embracing Forgiveness: Just as Christ offers forgiveness to those who repent, Christian spouses are called to extend grace and forgiveness to each other in times of relational conflict or betrayal (Colossians 3:13).

Conclusion

Adultery, from a Christian perspective, undermines the sanctity of marriage, disrupts God's design for relationships, and carries significant spiritual and relational consequences. By upholding fidelity, couples honor God, strengthen their marital bond, and reflect Christ's sacrificial love for His Church. Through prayer, Scripture study, and reliance on God's grace, Christian couples can navigate challenges, resist temptations, and cultivate a marriage that glorifies God—a testimony of His faithfulness and enduring love.